T0345041

Deploying the Zero Trust Framework in MSFT Azure

The Cloud is fast becoming the de facto standard for businesses in Corporate America today, with Microsoft Azure being one of the most widely used systems. However, given its stature, it has also become a prime target for the cyberattacker. Thus, a Zero Trust Framework is strongly needed. *Deploying the Zero Trust Framework in MSFT Azure* takes a closer look at the Cloud, the Zero Trust Framework, and how to deploy from both the technical and psychological perspectives.

Ravindra Das is a technical writer in the cybersecurity realm. He does cybersecurity consulting on the side through his private practice, RaviDas. Tech, Inc. He holds the Certified in Cybersecurity certification from the ISC2.

Cyber Shorts Series

Ransomware: Penetration Testing and Contingency Planning
Ravindra Das

Deploying the Zero Trust Framework in MSFT Azure
Ravindra Das

For more information about the series: https://www.routledge.com/Cyber-Shorts/book-series/CYBSH

Deploying the Zero Trust Framework in MSFT Azure

First Edition

Ravindra Das

CRC Press
Taylor & Francis Group
Boca Raton London New York

CRC Press is an imprint of the
Taylor & Francis Group, an **informa** business

Designed cover image: © ShutterStock Images

First edition published 2024
by CRC Press
2385 NW Executive Center Drive, Suite 320, Boca Raton FL 33431

and by CRC Press
4 Park Square, Milton Park, Abingdon, Oxon, OX14 4RN

CRC Press is an imprint of Taylor & Francis Group, LLC

ISBN: 978-1-032-58102-6 (hbk)
ISBN: 978-1-032-58101-9 (pbk)
ISBN: 978-1-003-44257-8 (ebk)

DOI: 10.1201/9781003442578

Typeset in Minion
by Deanta Global Publishing Services, Chennai, India

*This book is dedicated to my Lord and Savior,
Jesus Christ, the Grand Designer of the Universe, and
to my parents, Dr Gopal Das and Mrs Kunda Das.*

This book is also dedicated to:

Richard and Gwenda Bowman

Jaya Chandra

My loving cats, Fifi and Bubu

Contents

Acknowledgement

I would like to thank Ms Gabrielle Williams, my editor, who made this book a reality.

CHAPTER 1

The Cloud

INTRODUCTION

Today, many businesses are wondering whether or not to make the move to the Cloud, or whether or not to keep their On-Premises Infrastructure. As was mentioned in our previous book, *Ransomware: Penetration Testing and Contingency Planning*, the COVID-19 pandemic brought a lot of new changes upon the world, both good and bad. In terms of the latter, probably the worst news was the sheer number of deaths that occurred on a global basis.

Although all authoritative sources point to Wuhan province as being the prime area from which the COVID-19 virus first sprung, questions still remain whether it was simply a lab experiment that went bad or it was indeed spread from a meat market, populated with bats in the vicinity. But the common consensus here remains that if the Chinese government had simply shared any other information that they had at the time, a lot of these deaths could have been avoided.

As it was also reviewed, some of the good things that did happen were the following:

- The emergence of a near 99% remote workforce.

- A much quicker to time to develop and release much-needed vaccines.

DOI: 10.1201/9781003442578-1

- Cybersecurity issues were resolved in a quicker timeframe, despite new issues evolving over time. A perfect example of this was the intermeshing of both the home and corporate networks, and the consequences of Zoombombing.

But, as it was not mentioned in the last book, there were two new Cyber-related issues that were brought to the forefront as well because of the COVID-19 pandemic. First was the lack of contingency planning on the part of many Chief Information Security Officers (CISOs) (and even vCI-SOs) in Corporate America. For example, many of them did not even have an Incident Response Plan, Disaster Recovery Plan, or even a Business Continuity Plan put into place. Because of this, many businesses could not deploy a remote workforce in a quick and efficient manner because of a lack of this proper planning that was so badly needed.

Another side effect of this was that not every employee that was going to work remotely had a company-issued device with them in order to conduct their everyday job tasks. Because of this, and through no fault of their own, many of these kinds of employees had to resort to using their own devices in order to conduct their everyday job tasks. This put even more risk on the company, because these personal devices were not fitted with the proper security, encryption, and compliance mechanisms. Thus, the issue of Bring Your Own Device (BYOD) became even more prevalent.

The next subsection outlines some of the major Cyber threats that arise because of BYOD.

THE CYBER RISKS OF BYOD

1) The risks of corporate information being released:

> When an employee uses their own Smartphone to do their job tasks, there is a much greater chance that your trade secrets, intellectual property, or any other sensitive data could be released unknowingly, or even intercepted covertly by a third party. The primary reason for this is that employees very often do not keep their Smartphones up to date with the latest software patches and upgrades. Also, unencrypted network connections are used, such as public Wi-Fi hotspots. As a result, a cyberattacker can very easily tap into these insecure channels and steal your information and data.

2) Less control over personal wireless devices:

When a company issues its own Smartphones to its employees, there is some degree that the appropriate Security mechanisms will be implemented on them. This includes encryption, making sure that the devices are up to speed with the latest upgrades and patches, and that Two Factor Authentication (also known as 2FA) is installed. But, when an employee uses their own Smartphone or other wireless device to conduct their everyday job tasks, the business owner will then lose control over installing these protective mechanisms. After all, you cannot make an employee install them onto their own device if they do not want to. Because of this, 97% of BYOD devices have privacy issues, and 75% of them have inadequate data protection (Source: www.trilogytechnologies.com). Also, with a company-issued Smartphone, if an employee loses it, you can quickly and easily issue a Remote Wipe command. This will instantaneously delete all of the corporate information/data that resides on it. However, this command cannot be used with a Smartphone that belongs personally to the employee.

3) The mixing of personal and corporate data:

When an employee uses their own Smartphone, the risk their personal data being mixed in with corporate information and data becomes much greater. With this, there are increased chances that proprietary communications could be mistakenly sent to the wrong party. Also, there is a higher probability that malware or spyware could be covertly deployed onto the BYOD device, thus not only exposing proprietary corporate material, but your entire network as well. Keylogging software could also be installed by a cyberattacker, and as a result, they can also gain access to the usernames and passwords of your other employees.

THE MOBILE DEVICE MANAGEMENT PLAN

The other good thing that happened because of the COVID-19 pandemic was the development and implementation of not only the Incident Response Plan, the Disaster Recovery Plan, and the Business Continuity Plan (as CISOs now finally realized how important it was to have these in place and practiced in case there is a future pandemic yet to happen), but now CISOs also pay very close attention to what is known as also preparing a Mobile Device Management plan as well.

This was borne out because of the BYOD mishaps. Although a Mobile Device Management (MDM) plan will of course be very specific and unique to each and every business, there are certain benefits that it does bring to the table, some of these are as follows. But first, it is important to provide a technical definition of it:

> It is a tool that allows IT Administrators to centrally control, secure, and enforce policies on smartphones, tablets, notebooks, laptops, etc. and other wireless endpoints.

> *(Source: www.searchmobilecomuting.techtarget.com)*

The tool that is mentioned in the definition is actually a software package. It consists of an MDM server, and an MDM agent. The server component resides on the actual, main server that you use to conduct your day-to-day business operations. The MDM agent is a mobile app that is stored on the wireless devices that your employees possess.

All configurations, changes, etc. are done through a specialized console in the MDM server, and from there, with a few clicks of the mouse, these are then pushed out to all of the MDM agents. They, in turn, then automatically update all of the wireless devices. As you can see, the main advantage here is that of time savings, as everything is now centralized and can be done literally in just a matter of a few minutes.

The communication that takes place between the MDM server and the MDM agent is done through an Application Protocol Interface (API). This is integrated into the operating system (OS) of each wireless device. So, for example, the iOS that is on an iPhone and the Android OS that is on a Samsung will have their own API installed onto them.

THE BENEFITS OF A MOBILE DEVICE MANAGEMENT PLAN

The benefits that an MDM package can bring to your business are numerous, and include the following:

1) Device enrollment:

> As you hire a new employee, you do not have to physically access their device in order to enroll it into your network. This task can be

accomplished via the Over the Air (OTA) functionality. You can also quickly create customized user profiles for each of your employees.

2) Auditing capabilities:

You can obtain real-time information on a particular wireless device from anywhere you are. This is very useful in making sure that your employees are abiding by the Security policies you have set out. This functionality is very advantageous when it comes to password enforcement.

3) Device inventory and tracking:

You no longer have to keep a running list of all of your wireless devices on a spreadsheet, you can do all of this in the MDM server.

4) Monitoring functionalities:

You can monitor and keep track of all of the daily activities that take place on a wireless device from the date that it was first issued to the date when you retire it.

5) Remote wipe capability:

In case your employee loses their wireless device or in the event that it is stolen, you can quickly issue a Remote Wipe command. This will automatically erase all of the confidential information and data that reside on it.

THE COMPONENTS OF A GOOD MOBILE DEVICE MANAGEMENT PLAN

As just previously stated, crafting a good plan in this regard will depend a lot on your own security requirements of your business, just like the Incident Response Plan, Disaster Recovery Plan, and the Business Continuity Plan. But the following are some facets that you should give some serious consideration:

1) You first need to understand the requirements:

Yes, security is the main objective here, but you cannot buy an MDM package willy-nilly without considering what your company needs. Therefore, you need to include the following in the decision-making process:

- What are the kinds/types of wireless devices that your company will manage? For example, will it be just one brand or a mixture of them, such as iOS and Android?

- How many people really need a company-issued wireless device?

- What are the applications that your company will install on these wireless devices? Does the MDM software package come with tools to avoid Shadow IT Management?

2) Run the MDM in a sandboxed environment:

Once you have decided upon several MDM packages, it is imperative to test them out first, much like testing software code in a sandboxed environment before it is released into the production environment. In this case, the vendor you are working with should be able to provide you with a trial version of the package you are interested in. Install this onto numerous wireless devices, and see how it works, keeping the following as key points to be examined:

- How did the Multifactor Authentication (MFA) process go?

- How easy or convenient is it to "push" out company-wide applications? Does it happen in a relatively quick time, or does it take longer than anticipated?

- Can you configure the MDM package to the requirements outlined in your security policy?

- What built-in security features come with it? How easy is it to configure it?

It is essential to remember that the MDM package is tested on a wide range of devices in the OS. For example, run the software across the latest versions of the iOS and Android hardware. Ultimately, it needs to be able to interoperate well with the existing processes you have in your company. For example, if your remote employee is trying to access shared resources from the server from their wireless device, the software package should help to facilitate that process, not impede it.

3) Make sure that you have your back covered:

After you have thoroughly tested the MDM package, you are probably close to deciding which one you will procure. But before you do so, you have to be very careful of one thing: Make sure that the vendor you plan to purchase from has got you covered, especially from the standpoint of technical support. For example, if something fails in your MDM package, it could have a cascading effect on the other devices. Is the vendor available in situations like this to help you out quickly? Will they also keep you apprised of the latest patches and upgrades? What is the warranty plan like? Will the tech support be part of the original purchase contract, or will it come as a separate component? How responsive will they be in working with your IT Security team to weed out threats of Ransomware and other variants? These are vital questions to be asked and answered before the final decision is made. Remember that the cyberattacker will make wireless devices one of their top prey. You must ensure that your back is covered in this regard, as nobody else will do it. Finally, make sure that the MDM package you are considering purchasing comes with Remote Wipe functionality. This will let you delete everything off a wireless device in case it is lost or stolen.

4) Make sure you can access log files:

Data is the lifeblood of any business today, even for an MDM package. In this instance, you need to ensure that you can easily access all of the outputted log files or that there is some kind of central dashboard on which you can see them. The reason for this is that the log files provide a detailed history of how the MDM was used and accessed. In this regard, the log file can be a great tool to detect any suspicious behavior that is transpiring on your wireless network. It can also be used as forensics if your company falls victim to a security breach.

5) Control of data usage:

Of course, everybody wants to have unlimited data on their wireless device. But the more employees you have, the cost of this can significantly escalate. Your chosen MDM package should come with a feature that keeps track of the data usage across all of the wireless devices and automatically halts it in case of an unusual spike in activity. This is one of the first indicative signs that you could be in the middle of a security breach.

Also, it should notify you in case an employee is tampering with their wireless device to increase their data usage plan covertly.

An illustration of Mobile Device Management is below:

THE EVOLUTION OF CLOUD-BASED DEPLOYMENTS

One of the other good things that came out of the COVID-19 pandemic was the realization by both Corporate America and the CISOs was that it is extremely difficult to maintain On-Premises Infrastructure, if most of the employees are working remotely. Not only is it harder for the remote employees to gain access to the shared resources, but yet once again, the intermingling of both the corporate and home networks makes this proposition a very difficult one to act upon, because it simply opens too many back doors for the cyberattacker to penetrate. But apart from that, the next subsection clearly demonstrates some of the other pitfalls for a business to maintain On-Premises Infrastructure.

THE DISADVANTAGES OF ON-PREMISES INFRASTRUCTURE

Some of the following are reasons why it is not advantageous to have On-Premises Infrastructure:

1) It is too expensive:

Having 100% On-Premises Infrastructure is simply too costly. It comes down from many areas, but the bottom line is that when compared to Cloud deployment, it is simply just too expensive to maintain in the long run. And given the economic conditions of today as just described earlier in this chapter, it is really no longer viable for a business if it is to remain profitable for the long term.

2) More support is required:

In order to maintain 100% On-Premises Infrastructure, you are going to have to hire dedicated staff to just do that. For example, you will need to have administrators of all kinds (such as for the Database, the Servers, the Network, etc.), but you will also need to maintain a $24 \times 7 \times 365$ support team as well, in case your customers are having problems accessing their own personalized portals and accounts that reside on it. The bottom line here is that you are going to have much more expense in this regard, especially to pay your employees and to make them stay for the long term.

3) Greater need for compliance:

Every business in Corporate America that has a certain employee and/or revenue size, has to comply with the various Data Privacy laws such as that of the General Data Protection Regulation (GDPR), California Consumer Privacy Act (CCPA), Health Insurance Portability and Accountability Act (HIPAA), etc. But if you have 100% On-Premises Infrastructure, the hardware on which you store the Personally Identifiable Information (PII) datasets of both your customers and employees will also have to meet many compliance standards as well. Not only is it expensive to comply with the Data Privacy laws, but it will be even more if you have your own hardware and databases that store confidential information and data.

4) Higher levels of maintenance costs:

With 100% On-Premises Infrastructure, you and your IT Department will be primarily responsible for the costs that are associated with the upkeep of all of the hardware and software. Some examples of these include the costs to replace hardware as needed (especially if they have reached the proverbial "End of Life"), the costs that are associated with software licensing, and even procuring newer software application packages, the costs associated with software upgrades and patches, the installation of firmware, etc. Also keep in mind here that you will need extra staff to handle all of these tasks as well.

5) A greater capital expenditure:

With 100% On-Premises Infrastructure, you will have a greater cost to bear, which will have to be paid off over a period of time, and not all at once, which is where the operational expenditure concept comes into play. Having recurring expenses that are large can be detrimental to any company, no matter how much revenue that they may generate.

6) Increased chances of data loss:

With 100% On-Premises Infrastructure there are greater chances that your business will experience a data breach, or even a data exfiltration attack. The primary reason for this is that you will have to come up with your own set of controls and authentication mechanisms in order to protect your PII datasets. Not only will this take more time, but it will also drive up more cost in order to properly come up with and deploy these specific controls. Also, there will be maintenance costs as well, in order to keep your home-grown controls updated and also in compliance with the Data Privacy laws.

7) Scalability is highly limited:

If your business grows, so will the need to expand your IT and Network Infrastructure. This means that you will have to procure new hardware and software, but also have to hire the additional staff needed to maintain these new investments. Likewise, if your business suffers a downturn, you will need to scale back on your IT and Network Infrastructure. This simply means that whatever investments you made previously into your hardware and software will not be totally gone, thus causing a negative Return on Investment (ROI).

Because of these disadvantages and more, during the COVID-19 pandemic, many CISOs started to make a full migration to the Cloud, whether it was Amazon Web Services (AWS) or Azure (or even perhaps a combination of both). But the chief reason for this migration is that a Cloud-based deployment can fully support a near 99% remote workforce. It should be noted here that a migration to the Cloud means that the entire IT and Network Infrastructure is now entirely in AWS or Azure. An illustration of On-Premises Infrastructure is below:

A REVIEW OF THE CLOUD

Although one of our previous books, *Protecting Information Assets and IT Infrastructure in the Cloud, Second Edition,* gives very a detailed review of Cloud concepts, at this point it is important to highlight some of the key concepts again. First, we start defining what a Cloud deployment is. To many people it will have different meanings, but a technical definition of it is as follows:

> Cloud computing is the on-demand delivery of IT resources over the Internet with pay-as-you-go pricing. Instead of buying, owning, and maintaining physical data centers and servers, you can access technology services, such as computing power, storage, and databases, on an as-needed basis from a cloud provider like Amazon Web Services (AWS).

> *(Source: https://aws.amazon.com/what-is-cloud-computing/)*

So simply put, the Cloud is where you can access servers, workstations, and databases located at remote data centers located in different parts of the world, all through the Internet. While this may all sound simple, creating a Cloud-based deployment can be a complex process to undertake, but well worth it in the end.

THE THREE CLOUD PLATFORMS

When you are in the Cloud, you will hear of three very distinct terms, which are as follows:

1) The Infrastructure as a Service (the IaaS).

2) The Platform as a Service (the PaaS).

3) The Software as a Service (the SaaS).

We now examine these in more detail.

The Infrastructure as a Service

The technical definition for it is as follows:

> The Infrastructure-as-a-Service, commonly referred to as simply "IaaS", is a form of cloud computing that delivers fundamental compute, network, and storage resources to consumers on-demand, over the internet, and on a pay-as-you-go basis.
>
> *(Source: https://www.ibm.com/topics/iaas)*

In simpler terms, this is where one creates Virtual Machines, Virtual Desktops, Virtual Databases, etc. The disadvantage here is that you have little control over the resources that are built and deployed on this platform.

The Platform as a Service

The technical definition for it is as follows:

> The Platform as a service (PaaS) is a complete development and deployment environment in the cloud, with resources that enable you to deliver everything from simple cloud-based apps to sophisticated, cloud-enabled enterprise applications. You purchase the resources you need from a cloud service provider on a pay-as-you-go basis and access them over a secure Internet connection.
>
> Like IaaS, PaaS includes infrastructure—servers, storage, and networking—but also middleware, development tools, business intelligence (BI) services, database management systems, and

more. PaaS is designed to support the complete web application lifecycle: building, testing, deploying, managing, and updating.

(Source: https://azure.microsoft.com/en-us/resources/cloud -computing-dictionary/what-is-paas#:~:text=Platform%20as %20a%20service%20(PaaS,%2C%20cloud%2Denabled%20 enterprise%20applications)

While the PaaS also has the same infrastructure as the IaaS, the key difference here is that the end user also gets all of the tools they need in order to create, launch, and fully deploy a sophisticated, web-based application.

The Software as a Service

The technical definition for it is as follows:

Software-as-a-service (SaaS) is a form of cloud computing that delivers a cloud application—and all its underlying IT infrastructure and platforms—to end users through an internet browser. It can be an ideal solution for large enterprises, small businesses or individuals.

(Source: https://www.redhat.com/en/topics/cloud-computing/what -is-saas)

In simple terms, this is where your Cloud Provider (such as AWS or Azure) provides pre-built software applications that you purchase and use on an as-needed basis. All you have to do is merely configure the software application to your own environment and requirements.

The Serverless

This is a brand-new kind of Cloud platform, and the technical definition of it is as follows:

A serverless platform allows users to write and deploy code without the hassle of worrying about the underlying infrastructure.

(Source: https://www.cloudflare.com/learning/serverless/what-is -serverless/)

Since this is so new at the present time, the main kinds of customers for this kind of platform are the software developers. The main advantage here is that software applications can be created quickly without having to worry about managing the underlying infrastructure (which are the Virtual Machines, Virtual Desktops, Virtual Databases, etc.).

THE MAJOR CLOUD DEPLOYMENT MODELS

The last subsection reviews the major platforms that Cloud deployment can host. In other words, these are the pieces of infrastructure that can provide the support needed. But now, there are also the various Cloud deployment models, and the two of these should not be confused with each other. It is the Cloud deployment model which makes your infrastructure deliverable, and deliverable to your end users such as your employees and customers. There are three major types of Cloud deployment models, and they are as follows:

1) The Public Cloud:

   It can be technically defined as follows:

   The Public Cloud is an IT model where on-demand computing services and infrastructure are managed by a third-party provider and shared with multiple organizations using the public Internet. Public cloud service providers may offer cloud-based services such as infrastructure as a service (IaaS), platform as a service (PaaS), or software as a service (SaaS) to users for either a monthly or pay-per-use fee, eliminating the need for users to host these services on site in their own data center.

   (Source: https://www.vmware.com/topics/glossary/content/public-cloud.html)

   Probably the best example of this is when you open up a Cloud-based account on Azure. After it has been set up and provisioned, you can pretty much do anything you want or need to, which is creating Virtual Machines or Virtual Desktops. But keep in mind that although you will have the look and feel as if you are managing your own Cloud environment, you are actually sharing the same set of Cloud resources with other tenants on the same physical server. The only reason why you have this customized look is that your Cloud environment is hosted in a different logical partition.

2) The Private Cloud:

It can be technically defined as follows:

A private cloud is a cloud service that is exclusively offered to one organization. By using a private cloud, an organization can experience the benefits of cloud computing without sharing resources with other organizations. A private cloud can either be inside an organization or remotely managed by a third party and accessed over the Internet (but unlike a public cloud, it is not shared with anyone).

(Source: https://www.cloudflare.com/learning/cloud/
what-is-a-private-cloud/)

In other words, you get the same functionality and access to resources that you would get in the Public Cloud, but rather than sharing them with other tenants, you have your own, dedicated Cloud environment. But one of the downsides of this is that you become primarily responsible for managing it.

3) The Hybrid Cloud:

It can be technically defined as follows:

Hybrid cloud refers to a mixed computing, storage, and services environment made up of on-premises infrastructure, private cloud services, and a public cloud—such as Amazon Web Services (AWS) or Microsoft Azure—with orchestration among the various platforms. Using a combination of public clouds, on-premises computing, and private clouds in your data center means that you have a hybrid cloud infrastructure.

(Source: https://www.netapp.com/hybrid-cloud/
what-is-hybrid-cloud/)

This kind of Cloud-based deployment probably offers the most amount of flexibility, with the number of combinations that it has to offer. Some of these are as follows:

- Private Cloud—Public Cloud

- Private Cloud—On-Premises Infrastructure

- Public Cloud—On-Premises Infrastructure

- Private Cloud—Public Cloud—On-Premises Infrastructure

As was mentioned earlier in this chapter, many businesses in Corporate America have still been reluctant to migrate their entire IT and Network Infrastructure directly into the Cloud, for many numerous reasons. The Hybrid Cloud offers the best of both words for them, as they divide up one part of their IT and Network Infrastructure and put that either into a Public or Private Cloud deployment model, and leave the remaining components in their On-Premises Infrastructure.

THE BENEFITS OF THE CLOUD

When compared to On-Premises Infrastructure, the Cloud offers many benefits to its tenants. These are as follows:

1) Access anywhere, anytime:

With the Cloud, you and your employees and other third-party suppliers can gain access to all of the resources that you may need, anytime, anywhere in the world. All that is needed is a solid Internet connection, and of course that the appropriate permissions and authentication mechanisms have been assigned to everybody.

2) Get rid of all of the hardware and software:

With On-Premises Infrastructure, you are 100% responsible for the deployment, upkeep, and maintenance of your hardware and related software applications. But with the Cloud, all of that is done for you, and you have nothing to worry about. You can upgrade to the latest hardware and software applications as your needs and requirements dictate.

3) Data security is centralized:

Data privacy and data protection are some of the biggest issues today in Cyber environment. With On-Premises Infrastructure, you are responsible for all of that, and even complying with the Data

Privacy laws such as those of the GDPR, CCPA, and HIPAA. But when you move to the Cloud, all of this is managed for you in a centralized location. Also, the major Cloud Providers make available all of the tools you need, at no extra cost to you.

4) Higher levels of performance and availability:

With the Cloud, you sign a contract with your Cloud Provider, and one of these is known as the Service Level Agreement (SLA). This guarantees that all of your shared resources will be available on at least a 99.999% basis. If for some reason or another they are not at that guaranteed level, then your Cloud Provider will issue credits back to your account for the downtime experienced. But with On-Premises Infrastructure, you are primarily responsible for all of that. It can also be very problematic if your customers need to access their own portals and you are experiencing any kind or type of downtime.

5) Quicker time to deployment:

In today's world, creating web applications and other kinds of software applications in a quick timeframe is now a must. With the Cloud, you can now create and rapidly deploy software applications quicker than ever before. In fact, Azure even offers very specific tools to help you in this regard, as it relates to DevOps.

6) Business Insights:

With a Cloud-based deployment, you are provided with the tools to give you all kinds and types of analytics reports to give you updates on a real-time basis to give you an insight as to how your Cloud deployment is actually performing. Recommendations are even given as to how it can be improved, so that you get a quicker rate of ROI.

7) Business continuity is assured:

With On-Premises Infrastructure, you and your IT Department are primarily responsible for crafting the Incident Response Plan, the Disaster Recovery Plan, and the Business Continuity Plan. You even have to make sure that you have the right hardware, software, and backup facilities to restore your businesses mission-critical processes and operations as quickly as possible in case you are impacted by a security breach. But with a Cloud-based deployment, you don't have to worry at all about this. Many tools are provided to you in this regard, and with Azure, you can even replicate your entire IT and Network Infrastructure across multiple data centers in the different geographic regions throughout the entire world.

8) Cost savings:

As has been mentioned many times in this chapter, with On-Premises Infrastructure, you, the CISO, have full responsibility for the costs for the procurement, deployment, and maintenance of all of your hardware and software, and all of their upkeep. But with a Cloud-based deployment, not only is all of this done for you, but best of all, your costs have become very affordable, and you know what they will be upfront. For example, you will be charged on a monthly basis, a fixed flat fee. But of course, if you add on more resources, or scale them down, your price could then go up or down, respectively. The most important thing to keep in mind is that you are charged for only the cloud-based resources that you consume and use, nothing more and nothing less.

9) Scalability:

As was also mentioned in this chapter, if your business increases in terms of size, you will then need to scale up accordingly. With On-Premises Infrastructure, this can not only take a lot of time to accomplish, but it can also be an expensive proposition as well. But with the Cloud, this is all made very easy and very quick to deploy. For example, within minutes, you can add and deploy more Virtual Machines, Virtual Desktops, etc. By the same token, if you need to scale down, it is also very easy. With a Cloud-based environment, you will never even come close to the staggering costs that you would have with On-Premises Infrastructure.

10) More environmentally friendly:

With On-Premises Infrastructure, you and your IT Department are primarily responsible for disposing of old hardware. If not done properly, this can have grave consequences on the Earth's environment. But with a Cloud-based deployment, since everything is all virtualized, issues with contamination of the environment are not even a thought.

11) Security is enhanced:

With On-Premises Infrastructure, you are primarily responsible for the deployment of all of your security mechanisms and controls. But with a Cloud-based deployment, all of this for the most part is taken care of for you. Also, you are provided with the latest tools as well, to further configure your security environment. One such tool in Azure is known as Azure Sentinel.

12) Sharing of files:

With the 99% remote workforce of today, the sharing of files and instant collaboration is a must. With a Cloud-based deployment, this is all very easy and very quick to deploy as well.

In summary, the last subsection just reviewed some of the major benefits of a Cloud-based deployment. Of course, there are more, and in fact an entire white paper can be written just on that. But despite all of the advantages and security that a Cloud-based deployment has to offer, the cyberattacker is still targeting this, and there have been successful hacks and attacks on both the Azure and AWS environments. Because of this, the major Cloud Providers are now ramping up security even more, with the deployment of a newer methodology that is known as the "Zero Trust Framework". This is reviewed in some more detail in the next chapter.

CHAPTER 2

A Review of the Zero Trust Framework

INTRODUCTION

As we all know today, literally everything that is out there in the world today is prone to a cyberattack, whether it is digital or physically based in nature. As it has been examined many times, not only in this book, but past ones that we have published as well, we are all—both individuals and businesses alike—prone to becoming a victim of a cyberattack. In the end, there is really no way around this at all.

The only thing that we can do as a society is to try to make ourselves as immune as possible from this actually happening to us. In other words, in the techno jargon of Cybersecurity, we need to take steps to mitigate the risks of this happening. For example, we make use of all of the technology, tools, and gadgets that we can ever imagine, but none of that will mean anything if we do not take a proactive stance in doing so.

Being proactive simply means that we are cognizant of our surroundings on a daily basis. Being proactive also means trusting and listening to our gut feelings if something is right or not. Being proactive also means that we report to the authorities if we witness anything that is suspicious or abnormal that is happening. Remember that in the end, taking a good proactive stance also means that we use both human intervention and technology to stay one step ahead of the cyberattacker. We don't go too much in either extreme.

DOI: 10.1201/9781003442578-2

But unfortunately, at the present time, it is the cyberattacker that is ahead of the game, despite all of our efforts to try to stay ahead in the proverbial "cat and mouse game". In response to this, Corporate America has now started to adopt a new Cybersecurity Framework that is known as the "Zero Trust Framework". Its basic theme is that nobody should be trusted, and everybody must be verified at all times and instances when wishing to gain access to a shared resource, or private and confidential information and data.

We now take a closer look at this. But before we do that, it is important that we look at some of the other security models that have evolved over time. After all, it is the goal of the Zero Trust Framework to supersede all of them, if at all possible.

THE CYBERSECURITY MODELS

At the present time, there are four main Cybersecurity Models, not including the Zero Trust Framework. They are as follows:

- The Lockheed Martin Cyber Kill Chain.

- The Diamond Model of Intrusion Analysis.

- The MITRE ATT&CK Model.

- Perimeter Defense Model.

THE LOCKHEED MARTIN CYBER KILL CHAIN

This Cybersecurity Model was actually developed by the giant defense contractor known as Lockheed Martin. It has probably been around for the longest time, having been first published in 2011. Its basic premise is to outline the specific steps that a cyberattacker would take from creating a threat variant, launching it, and taking whatever they have targeted in return. In most instances, it would be the Personally Identifiable Information (PII) datasets of businesses. The steps of the Cyber Kill Chain Model include the following:

1) Reconnaissance:

   In this first step, the cyberattacker is scouting their unsuspecting victim in order to determine their particular vulnerabilities, gaps, and weaknesses that can be easily penetrated. In this regard, the cyberattacker will take all the time they need, they are in no particular rush to take action. Most of the tools that are used in this regard include Social Media sites, Open Source Intelligence (OSINT), and even conducting paid background checks that are widely available now on the Internet. Also, Social Engineering can be used in this regard in order to trick employees into giving out confidential information and data about their place of employment. Typically, these kinds of attacks are conversational in nature, and can take time to build up the trust and rapport.

2) Weaponization:

Once the victim has been decided upon, the cyberattacker now chooses the threat variant from which they will launch their attack, and how it will be armed, also technically referred to as "Weaponization". This can be anything from Ransomware, Trojan Horses, to Worms, Viruses, Phishing, etc., you name it.

3) Delivery:

This is where the malicious payload has been delivered. But it is important to keep in mind here that once the victim and the arsenal have been decided upon by the cyberattacker, the delivery part of this model does not happen immediately. For example, once the cyberattacker has penetrated their target, they tend to like to stay in for long periods of time, going unnoticed. Once they become satisfied in this regard, they will then deploy the malicious payload in the most covert way possible.

4) Exploitation:

At this stage of the game, the cyberattacker then takes full advantage of any further weaknesses, gaps, or vulnerabilities that they have discovered while they were in their victim. This is technically known as "Exploitation".

5) Installation:

If the first rounds of Exploitation have been successful, then the cyberattacker will think about looking for new gaps, weaknesses, and vulnerabilities, and deploying more malicious payloads. Essentially this becomes a repeat of steps 1–4 all over again.

6) Command and Control:

In many of the cyberattacks of today, the cyberattacker actually launches their attacks and deploys the malicious payload from a remote location. The device(s) that is (are) used for this can actually take over and control the victimized device at this point.

7) Actions On Objectives:

At this point, the cyberattacker, if they are well prepared enough, will then evaluate what they have done, learn from any mistakes made, apply what they have learned, and from there, move onto the next unsuspecting victim.

DIAGRAM OF THE LOCKHEED MARTIN KILL CHAIN MODEL

This entire chain of events is illustrated below:

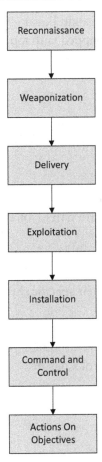

As one can see from the above illustration, the Cyber Kill Chain Model takes a very linear approach towards the analysis of a cyberattack that has taken place. While this model has the primary advantage of having been around for a long period of time, its main disadvantage is that Cybersecurity analysts that use it can greatly oversimplify a cyberattack and make rash and quick conclusions.

THE DIAMOND MODEL OF INTRUSION ANALYSIS

This Cyber Model made its first appearance back in 2006, it was not published in the scientific journals until 2013. Sergio Caltagirone, Andrew Pendergrast, and Christopher Betz created it. The main purpose of this Cyber Model is to not take a linear approach to analyzing a cyberattack, but instead to focus on the specific cyberattacker behaviors and identify the relationships between the cyberattacker's motivations, the victim, and the technology/tools used to launch a cyberattack.

But rather than taking a straight linear approach, the model makes use of the shape of a diamond, mapped with four distinct quadrants. They are as follows:

1) The Adversary:

> This is the actual cyberattacker themselves, along with their behavior and personality traits.

2) The Infrastructure:

> These are typically the digital assets which include, for example, TCP/IP addresses, domain names, or email addresses.

3) Capabilities:

> The strengths and the advantages that the cyberattacker has when it comes to launching their specific threat variants.

4) The Victim:

> These are the typically the humans, businesses, or even the IT and Network Infrastructure of a business.

DIAGRAM OF THE DIAMOND MODEL OF INTRUSION ANALYSIS

This model is illustrated below:

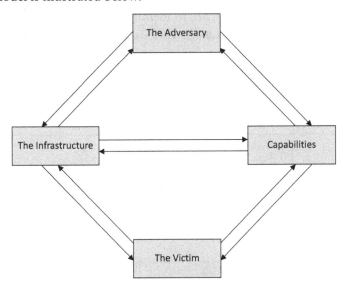

A goal of this Cybersecurity model is to get as granular as possible as it relates to the relationship between the cyberattacker and their victim. Another major objective of the Diamond Model was to also closely examine the nature of what is known as "Pivoting".

With the process of Pivoting, researchers can identify ways to launch an attack in certain environments that literally have no defense mechanisms. A lot of "Noise" can also be created in this process. It is hoped that these Noises can be used to determine the elusive intentions of the cyberattacker. Pivoting can be examined by closely scrutinizing the relationships between the cyberattacker, the Target Infrastructure, and the defense mechanisms of the victim.

The Diamond Model of Intrusion Detection allows for Cybersecurity Researchers to identify and confirm the relationships between the various attack vectors. The focus is not so much on the components but on their interrelationships with one another.

Also, various kinds and types of Activity Groups can be created as well. This allows Cybersecurity Researchers to examine and map the steps of a cyberattack throughout the entire attack.

THE ATTACK GRAPHS

This is a combination of both the Cyber Kill Chain Model and the Diamond Model of Intrusion Analysis. This newer methodology allows for the Cybersecurity Researcher to identify each step of the Cyber Kill Chain Model, but also examine the various Pivot Points that the cyberattacker takes from within those specific steps. In fact, the Attack Graphs have formed the foundation for the theoretical concepts of Intrusion Detection and Threat Hunting.

DIAGRAM OF THE ATTACK GRAPHS MODEL

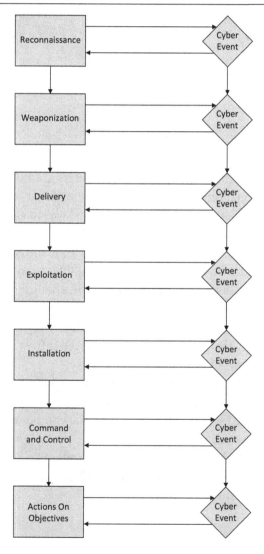

THE MITRE ATT&CK MODEL

This is an acronym that stands for the "Adversarial Tactics, Techniques, and Common Knowledge" Model. Just like the Lockheed Martin Kill Chain Model, this model follows a number of sequential steps from the inception of the cyberattack to its launch. These steps are as follows:

1) Initial Access:

   This is when the cyberattacker first makes penetration into the victim and stays in for however long that they think it is necessary to deploy the malicious pieces of payload.

2) Execution:

   This is where the malicious payload is actually launched into the IT and Network Infrastructure of a business, and does the task it was designed to do, which is most likely data exfiltration of some kind or type.

3) Persistence:

   If the first hack has been successful, then the cyberattacker will try repeated attempts to penetrate the target through other forms of gaps, weaknesses, and vulnerabilities that are present.

4) Privilege Escalation:

   Another area in which the cyberattacker can cause damage is trying to gain access to Privileged Accounts, which are essentially "super user" accounts that managers of both the IT Department and IT Security team use to gain access to mission-critical operations.

5) Defense Evasion:

   If new weaknesses, gaps, or vulnerabilities have been found and have been penetrated, the cyberattacker will then come up with new ways in order to appear covert and hide their tracks so that they cannot be detected.

6) Credential Access:

   This is also similar to Privilege Escalation, but rather in this instance, the cyberattacker is also trying to gain access to the other login credentials that are used by employees. So, this can be used as a two-pronged attack, if the cyberattacker also has access to any sort of Privileged Access.

7) Discovery:

This is where the cyberattacker finds new targets to hit on to deploy the malicious payload, based upon new vulnerabilities, gaps, and weaknesses that were also discovered.

8) Lateral Movement:

Rather than move in a linear fashion like the Lockheed Martin Kill Chain Model suggests is what typically happens, in this instance, the cyberattacker moves in a lateral fashion, from one place to another in the IT and Network Infrastructure. This is one of the better ways that the cyberattacker can move about without being detected at first glance by the IT Security team. This kind of technique is also used commonly in a newer threat vector that is known as Advanced Persistent Threats (APTs).

9) Collection:

At this particular phase, the cyberattacker takes a moment to pause and evaluates all that they have done thus far, from steps 1–8. If he or she deems that they have been successful, they will then move on by repeating steps all over again.

10) Command and Control:

This is also one of the same steps that is in the Lockheed Martin Kill Chain Model. This is where the cyberattacker penetrates their target from a remote position, and from there also launches the malicious payload to do whatever nefarious acts that it has been created to do.

Finally, it should be noted that the MITRE ATT&CK Model actually maps out and details specific tactics and procedures with each of the above-mentioned steps. Further, with this kind of model, one can map out the specific tactics and procedures to real world cyberattacker groups. From here, you can further identify common techniques and procedures that the cyberattacker could use when they target your business.

Weaponization.

Delivery.

Exploitation.

Installation.

Command and Control.

Actions on Objectives.

THE PERIMETER DEFENSE MODEL

The truth is that the abovementioned models are more or less theoretical in nature, and it is quite possible that not a lot of businesses in Corporate America have made actual, heavy usage of them. But there is one type of model that most businesses have actually made use of, and this is technically known as the "Perimeter Defense Model". To understand this better, let us illustrate this with an example. Suppose that you are on an island, and the actual geography of the land is circular. But surrounding all of this land is a vast pool of water, such as the ocean, whether it is the Atlantic or Pacific.

This is what is giving your primary means of defense. In the end, who would want to enter this island that you are on by having to traverse across the rough ocean waters? Well, there is one kind of person or group that would possibly do this, and this is the cyberattacker. Of course, they would make every attempt possible to come onto your island, especially if it had great treasure or other such highly valuable items.

But to protect your island, you have also laid various defense mechanisms to fend off anybody from coming onto the land. For example, you may have a system of guns or other kinds of weapons, or if there is a population on your island, it is quite likely also that you could have enlisted others to serve as guards or even soldiers to add to that protection around your island.

But now, keep in mind that all of your defenses are on the shore of your island, which are the guards, and other artillery that you have may enlisted the use of. But suppose that an attacker, or an invader, was not only able to cross the ocean to get to your riches, but that they were also able to infiltrate all of your lines of defense on the shore of your island? They could have done this covertly, or they simply could have launched some kind of brute force attack in order to take out all of your defenses, or at least just enough so that they could break through one area of vulnerability, and from there take over the entire island.

Once they have broken through, the invaders now have complete and unfettered access to everything that is on this piece of land. By this point, you may be wondering, how on Earth did this happen? Well, the bottom line is that because the invaders were able to break through your first and only line of defense, they were able to take control over your entire territory, and steal whatever they could, which would most likely be all of your assets.

But now, what if you had adopted a layered approach to protecting your island? Well, if this methodology was applied then the invaders would have had to break through multiple lines of defenses. Because of this, either they would have run out of ammunition, or they would have given up in complete exhaustion. This leads to what is known as the "Zero Trust Framework", and this is discussed in the next subsection of this chapter.

The model as just illustrated is typically how most businesses have adopted their approaches to Cybersecurity. Now while there may not be a completely visible circle surrounding the business, there is only one line of defense. It is through this one line of defense only that actually separates the internal and external environments of the business. The former will of course contain the IT and Network Infrastructure, while the latter would be all of the variables impacting the (either for the good or bad) business from the outside.

This can also be compared to the island example once again. The land on which you live (as well as the other tenants) is considered to be the internal environment, and the ocean (such as the Pacific or the Atlantic) that surrounds your island is the external environment. From here, all of the elements from the water and the sky will impact where you are situated. The same is true of the Perimeter Defense Model, where all sorts of threat variants from the external environment are waiting for their golden moment in which to penetrate.

But as it relates to Cybersecurity, the Perimeter Defense is where a particular business will put all of its defense mechanisms. For example, these have traditionally been the network security devices, such as the Network Intrusion Devices, Hubs, Routers, Firewalls, etc. But the problem here, as one can see, if all of these devices were just implemented and deployed just at this very line only, if the cyberattacker were to break through them, then they would have free reign over everything that is digital or even physically related at your place of business.

In this regard, there has been a common misunderstanding amongst Chief Information Security Officers (CISOs) is that the more you can put on this one line of defense, the better. While in theory this may sound plausible, the truth of the matter is that it is a very poor way of implementing Cybersecurity. The primary reason for this is that by taking this approach, it is more than likely you will be deploying newer security tools and technologies from many different vendors. This will not only increase the attack surface of your business, but by having too many discrepant devices will also create different log output files, which your IT Security team also has to analyze. By having to go through so much, this leads to a huge problem that is called "Alert Fatigue". So, if your business is one that still relies heavily upon the Perimeter Defense Model, then you as the CISO, and your IT Security team need to conduct an exhaustive Risk Assessment study of not only of your digital and physical assets, but also of your Cyber defense tools and other sorts of mechanisms. Then from there, you need strategically to determine how to reorganize these defense mechanisms. For example, they need to be placed where they are needed the most, and the locations that are the most vulnerable at your place of business.

You should try this approach first rather than procuring and deploying newer security technologies in a haphazard fashion. The bottom line here is that it is probably better to use only three firewalls if they are strategically placed versus the ten brand-new ones placed haphazardly. But finally, for you as the CISO, it is very important for you to get away from the line of thinking from the old proverb that there is "Safety in Numbers". In the world of Cybersecurity, this simply does not exist at all.

The Perimeter Defense Model is illustrated below:

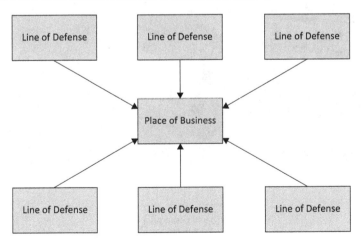

UNIMODAL AUTHENTICATION

It should be noted that in the Perimeter Defense Model, only one means of authentication and/or authorization is actually used. This is the traditional username/password combination, a PIN Number etc. This is known as the "Unimodal" approach to Cybersecurity, because only one type of authentication is actually used. But, as we have all seen, the password is easy penetrable, no matter how long or complex it is.

As a result, this has given birth to a sort of newer approach to Cybersecurity, which is known as Two Factor Authentication (2FA). This is reviewed in the next subsection.

TWO FACTOR AUTHENTICATION

Because of the grave security vulnerabilities with the Unimodal approach, a newer methodology was conceived of. In this situation, an end user has to present two forms of authentication in order to be granted access to the shared resources. The first round could be the traditional username/password combination, and the second layer of authentication could be a challenge/response question, or even a Personal Identification Number (PIN). The 2FA approach is most commonly used when it comes to accessing the shared resources server. This is illustrated in the diagram below:

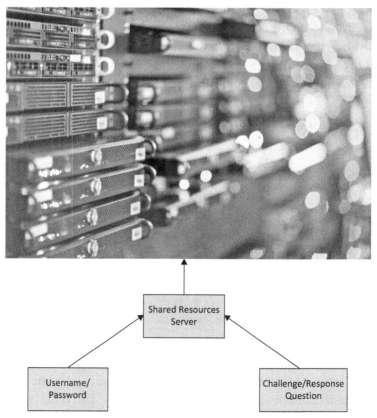

It should be noted that in these kinds of scenarios, it is best to make sure that 2FA is as robust as possible and make sure that the authentication mechanisms follow the process in a sequential order. For example, first would come the username/password, then immediately after will come the challenge/response question. But once again, the use of 2FA has also shown its flaws, just like the Unimodal approach. The primary reason for this is that with the tools that are available today, a cyberattacker can very easily crack these traditional mechanisms very quickly.

MULTIFACTOR AUTHENTICATION

This is deemed to be the best method possible at the present time for confirming the identity of an individual. In this scenario, at least three or even more layers of authentication are used before the end user can gain access to the shared resources. This once again could be the username/password, the challenge/response question, and even an RSA Token. This is illustrated in the diagram below:

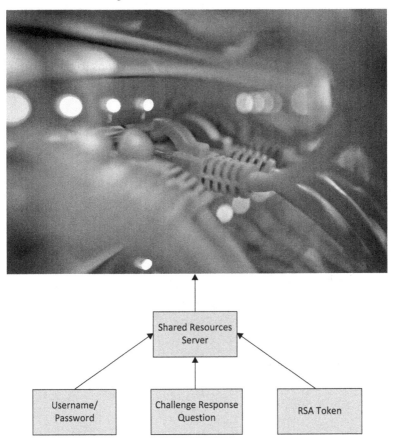

As just mentioned, even more layers of authentication can be used. Of course, the more you have the better. But in the illustration above, there is still one inherent weakness, just like the 2FA approach. That is, even the types of authentication mechanisms illustrated can also be broken through by the cyberattacker. So, is there another option for this? Yes, and the answer lies in the use of Biometrics, which is discussed in the next subsection.

USING BIOMETRICS IN MULTIFACTOR AUTHENTICATION

Biometrics is the science of confirming your identity based upon the unique physical and/or characteristics about yourself. Specifically, it can be defined as follows:

> Biometrics are unique physical characteristics, such as fingerprints, that can be used for automated recognition. At the Department of Homeland Security, biometrics are used for detecting and preventing illegal entry into the U.S., granting and administering proper immigration benefits, vetting and credentialing, facilitating legitimate travel and trade, enforcing federal laws, and enabling verification for visa applications to the U.S.
>
> *(Source: https://www.dhs.gov/biometrics)*

There are two groupings of Biometrics, which are as follows:

1) Physical Biometrics

These include the following:

- Fingerprint Recognition.

- Vein Pattern Recognition.

- Facial Recognition.

- Iris Recognition.

- Retinal Recognition.

- Voice Recognition.

2) Behavioral Biometrics

These include the following:

- Signature Recognition.

- Keystroke Recognition.

While in theory all of these above Biometric technologies could possibly be used in a Multifactor Authentication (MFA) scenario, at the present time, it is only Iris Recognition, Facial Recognition, and Fingerprint Recognition that are used the most. The primary reason for this that these modalities are proven to work when and where needed, and have a strong level of user acceptance, which is of the utmost importance when it comes to adopting and using Biometric Technology.

Probably the biggest reason why Biometrics is starting to gain attention is that it possesses a number of key advantages, which are as follows:

- It offers an almost bulletproof method of confirming the identity of an individual.

- It is very difficult to replicate, as each person has their own unique set of physical and/or behavioral traits.

- The raw images that are captured by a Biometric system get converted into a mathematical file. For example, the raw images from a Fingerprint Recognition system become a binary mathematical file, the raw images that come from an Iris Recognition device get converted into templates that are designed by Gabor Wavelet mathematics, and the raw images that are collected from a Facial Recognition system become Hidden Markov Models, which are high level statistical-based profiles. So, if a cyberattacker were to heist a Biometric Template (which are the mathematical files as just described), there is hardly anything that one can do with them. After all, it is not the same as stealing a credit card number and making fraudulent purchases from it.

- Biometric Templates are very easy to reset, unlike passwords, and there is very often a cost that is associated with them (the current number point is at least $400.00 per employee per year).

But it should be noted here that if you are using Biometrics in a MFA approach, you should use them for all of the authentication mechanisms, in rapid succession. This is illustrated in the example below:

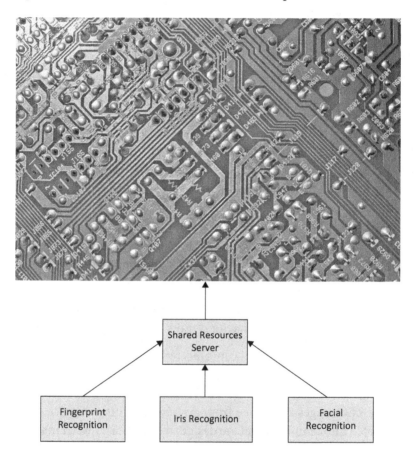

Since all of these are very unique authentication mechanisms, in the view of the author, this is the best route to take when deploying a MFA solution. This brings up a very important point. All of the authentication mechanisms that are used (no matter what methodology you make use of, 2FA or MFA) all of the authentication mechanisms must be different from each other. In other words, you should not use (as an example) the username/password combination twice in a sequential fashion. It is this MFA approach that drives the Zero Trust Framework, which is reviewed in the next subsection.

THE ZERO TRUST FRAMEWORK

This model totally does away with the traditional Perimeter Defense Model. With this newer approach, the main mantra here is to "Never Trust, Always Verify". As has been stated in this book thus far, with this approach, absolutely nobody is to be trusted. This even includes those employees that have been with you for the longest time. In this particular methodology, whenever anybody wants to gain access to shared resources, they must be verified each and every time. True, this can become quite exhaustive in the end, so the Zero Trust Framework allows for the use of both Artificial Intelligence (AI) and Machine Learning (ML) to automate these processes.

A typical example here is for Privileged Access Accounts, and this is reviewed in great detail as it relates to the Zero Trust Framework in our previous book, *The Zero Trust Framework: Threat Hunting and Quantum Mechanics*. Apart from the constant verification theme, another main objective of the Zero Trust Framework is to divide up the IT and Network Infrastructure into smaller zones, or segments. As it relates to networking, this is also technically known as "Subnetting". In this instance, each piece of digital asset becomes its own island, with its own layers of defense, which is that of the MFA, as just reviewed. So rather than having the entire IT and Network Infrastructure as one huge island, the goal here now is to have much smaller islands, each with its own layer of defense.

The objective here is to theoretically create an infinite amount of defense layers ahead of the proverbial crown jewels of the company. So, if the cyberattacker were to break through one layer of defense, the chances of them breaking through the rest becomes statistically zero. A simple illustration of the Zero Trust Framework is below:

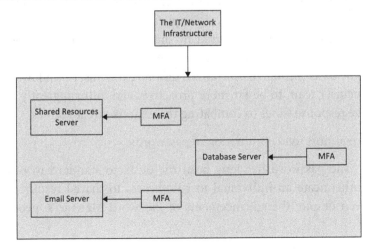

THE ADVANTAGES OF THE ZERO TRUST FRAMEWORK

When compared to the traditional Perimeter Defense Model, the Zero Trust Framework offers a number of key advantages, which are as follows:

1) A much greater level of accountability:

When the Remote Workforce started to take off 2022 because of COVID-19, many companies were in a rush to issue company devices. Unfortunately, not every business entity could do this, and as a result of this, employees were forced to use their own devices in order to conduct their daily job tasks. But this also triggered a whole new host of security issues. As organizations are starting to implement the concept of Zero Trust, there is now a much higher degree of accountability of which devices are being used in this regard. For example, if an employee wishes to gain access to corporate resources on their own device, they can no longer do so, as they now must use company-issued equipment which possess these authentication mechanisms so that access can be granted.

2) It facilitates the use of centralized monitoring:

When security tools and technologies are used in different combinations with no planning in mind, it can be very difficult for the IT Security team to keep track of all of the warnings and alerts that are coming in. This can make it very difficult to triage and escalate the real Cyber threats that are out there. But with the Zero Trust methodology, since each and every device is accounted for in a logical manner, a centralized approach can now be utilized. One typical example of this is what is known as the Security Incident and Event Management software application. With this, not only can the false positives be filtered by making use of both AI and ML, but the legitimate warnings and alerts can be presented on a real-time basis through a centralized dashboard. Thus, this allows the IT Security team to be far more proactive, and in turn, greatly reduce the response times to combating the various threat vectors.

3) An almost total elimination of passwords:

The password has long been the de facto standard in order to authenticate an individual to gain access to shared resources. But even despite the advancements of Password Managers, people are still stuck in their old ways, making passwords even more vulnerable than they were ever before. With the Zero Trust Framework, much greater efforts are now taken to totally eradicate the use of passwords and use much more robust authentication tools. For example, there is now a heavy reliance upon using Biometric Technology. With this, a unique physiological or behavioral trait is extracted from the individual in order to 100% confirm their identity, which obviously nobody else possesses. The biggest advantage of this is that different kinds and types of Biometric modalities (such as Fingerprint Recognition, Iris Recognition, Facial Recognition, etc.) can be implemented at different points in the corresponding security layers. For example, they can be used individually, and in tandem with each other to create a very secure environment.

4) Scalability is offered:

With the Remote Workforce now guaranteed to be a long-term phenomenon, many companies are now opting to make greater usage of Cloud-based resources, such as those offered by Amazon Web Services (AWS) or Microsoft Azure. There are of course those entities that still choose to have a bricks-and-mortar presence, and to a certain degree still have some remnants of an On-Premises solution. But whatever option is chosen, the Zero Trust Framework allows for the seamless transfer for apps, digital assets, and even the confidential information and data (especially the PII datasets) from one place to another in a much more secure fashion.

5) Breaking in becomes close to impossible:

Before the COVID-19 pandemic hit, many businesses adopted what is known as the "Perimeter Security" approach to protecting their digital assets. This simply means that there was only one line of defense separating the internal environment from the external environment. As a result, if the cyberattacker were to penetrate through this, they could gain access to just about anything in the IT and Network Infrastructure and move covertly in a lateral fashion. But with the Zero Trust Framework, the implementation of multiple layers of security means that it becomes that much harder for the cyberattacker to gain access to the proverbial "Crown Jewels", as it will take much longer to break through each and every line of defense as they try to go in deeper. In the end, more than likely, he or she will just give up.

6) Greater adherence to compliance:

With the heightened enforcement of the General Data Protection Regulation (GDPR), California Consumer Privacy Act (CCPA), Health Insurance Portability and Accountability Act (HIPAA), etc., companies now have to comply with all of the various statutes and provisions that are applicable to them. By adopting the Zero Trust Framework, businesses will now be assured of keeping up that level of compliance, as they will be forced now to implement the right set of controls (which are essentially the authentication mechanisms) in order to protect their PII datasets, which is what is being scrutinized the most by auditors and regulators.

HOW TO DEPLOY THE ZERO TRUST FRAMEWORK

At this point, it is very important to keep in mind that deploying the Zero Trust Framework is not a "one size fits all" approach. Rather, it is unique to the environment of each and every business, and a lot depends upon your own security requirements. The following are some guidelines, that you, the CISO, need to take into consideration when pondering the merits of deploying the Zero Trust Framework in your business:

1) Understand and completely define what needs to be protected:

With Zero Trust, you don't assume that your most vulnerable digital assets are at risk. Rather, you take the position that everything is prone to a security breach, no matter how minimal it might be to your company. In this regard, you are taking a much more holistic view, in that you are not simply protecting what you think the different potential attack plans could be, but you are viewing this as an entire surface that needs 100% protection, on a $24 \times 7 \times 365$ basis. So, you and your IT Security team need to take a very careful inventory of everything digital that your company has, and from there, mapping out how each of them will be protected. So rather than having the mindset of one overarching line of defense for your business, you are now taking the approach of creating many different "Micro Perimeters" for each individual asset.

2) Determine the interconnections:

In today's environment, your digital assets are not just isolated to themselves. For example, your primary database will be connected with others, as well as to other servers, which are both physical and virtual in nature. Because of this, you also need to ascertain how these linkages work with one another, and from there, determine the types of controls that can be implemented in between these digital assets so that they can be protected.

3) Crafting the Zero Trust Framework:

It is important to keep in mind that instituting this does not take a "one size fits all" approach. Meaning, what may work for one company will not work for your business. The primary reason for this is that not only do you have your own unique set of security requirements, but the protection surface (as defined in step #1) and the linkages that you have determined (defined in step #2) will also be unique to you as well. Therefore, you need to adopt the mindset that you need to create your framework tailored to what your needs are at that moment in time, as well as considering projected future needs as well.

4) Drafting the Security Policies:

Once you have determined what your overall Zero Trust Framework will look like, you then need to create the Security Policies that will go along with it. For example, it will be very detailed and granular in nature, given the "Micro Perimeters" approach that the Zero Trust Framework uses. So, you will need to determine the following for each and every digital asset that you have mapped out (which was accomplished in step #1):

- Who the end-users are (this will be your employees, contractors, outside third-party vendors and suppliers, etc.).

- The types of shared resources that they will be accessing on a daily basis.

- What those specific access mechanisms will be.

- The security mechanisms (particularly the controls) that will be used to protect that level of access.

5) Implement how the Zero Trust Framework will be determined:

Once you have accomplished steps #1–4, the final goal to be achieved is how it will be monitored on a real-time basis. In this particular instance, you will want to make use of what is known as a Security Information and Event Management (SIEM) software package. This is an easy tool to deploy that will collect all of the logging and activity information, as well as all of the warnings and alerts and put them into one central view. The main advantage of this is that your IT Security team will be able to triage and act upon those threat variants almost instantaneously.

In our next chapter, we examine some of the high-level principles of implementing the Zero Trust Framework in Microsoft Azure.

CHAPTER 3

Deploying the Zero Trust Framework in Azure

INTRODUCTION

At the present time, there are three main Cloud juggernauts, and they are as follows:

1) Amazon Web Services.

2) Microsoft Azure.

3) Google Cloud Platform.

All of these Cloud Providers have their own very unique way of offering products and services to their customers, but at the present time, in the view of the author, it is Microsoft Azure that offers the most robust package when it comes to deploying the Zero Trust Framework. But as reviewed in one of our previous books: *Protecting Information Assets and IT Infrastructure in the Cloud, Second Edition*, there are many, many moving parts to Azure, and to cover how the Zero Trust Framework can be applied to each, and one of them is far beyond the scope of this book.

But instead, we will take a closer look at the overall methodology that Azure has embraced for the Zero Trust Framework when it comes to offering this to their tenants.

DOI: 10.1201/9781003442578-3

HOW THE ZERO TRUST FRAMEWORK IS EMBRACED BY MICROSOFT AZURE

The Zero Trust Framework in Azure is viewed as the means to which

> every access request is strongly authenticated, authorized within policy constraints and inspected for anomalies before granting access. Everything from the user's identity to the application's hosting environment is used to prevent breach.
>
> *(Source: "Zero Trust Maturity Model", white paper by Microsoft)*

To this extent, there are three major components to the Zero Trust Framework as it relates to Azure:

1) Explicit Verification:

As was mentioned in the last chapter, each and every employee must be verified for anything they want to or need to access in order to conduct their daily job tasks. There is no doubt that this can become cumbersome over time, so the use of Artificial Intelligence (AI) and Machine Learning (ML) are typically used to help automate some of these processes. In fact, Azure has some great AI tools that can be used for this very purpose, through the business relationship that it has with OpenAI. An extensive review of this has been provided in our previous book, *Protecting Information Assets and IT Infrastructure in the Cloud, Second Edition.*

2) Making use of Least Privilege:

This is one of the key components of the Zero Trust Framework in general. With this concept in hand, you only want to give your employees just enough rights, privileges, and permissions that they need to do their jobs. The fundamental concept here is that you don't want to give out too little or too much, as any extreme like this can create back doors for the cyberattacker to easily penetrate.

3) Assuming the worst-case scenario:

One of the cardinal rules in Cybersecurity is that you cannot assume that you are safe, not even in the slightest. So with this in mind, you must always assume that there are strong chances that a cyberattacker is actually lurking within your Azure Cloud deployment. By assuming this posture, you will:

- Prevent lateral movement by the cyberattacker.

- Ensure that all of your endpoints are made secure with the highest levels of Encryption that Azure has to offer.

- Adopt a proactive security mindset which includes the real-time monitoring of log files outputted by the network security devices which you have deployed in Azure. Once again, this can be a very cumbersome task if one of your employees were to do it, but Azure has both AI and ML tools to automate these processes for you.

THE USE OF POLICIES

One of the tools that Azure has in its arsenal to help you deploy the Zero Trust Framework is what is known as the "Azure Policy Manager". This has been designed to help your business to overcome the day-to-day hurdles that you could experience with your Zero Trust Framework deployment. This can be used for the following kinds of tasks:

- Fine tune your access and authentication policies.

- The above can be applied to the most granular levels of employee geographic location, the type of device that they are using, and even the software applications that they are accessing from within Azure.

- Getting real-time snapshots as to how your backend systems (such as your Azure Databases) are interacting with the front end (which would be your Azure Virtual Machines).

- Be able to implement what is known as Role-Based Access Control (RBAC) in a much more effective and efficient manner into the Azure Active Directory.

- How to better approach your practice of deploying your Multifactor Authentication (MFA) mechanism. In this regard, Azure has a plethora of tools that you can use to deploy an MFA framework in just a matter of a few minutes, even including the use of Biometric Technology, which was reviewed in the last chapter.

WHAT IS INCLUDED IN THE AZURE ZERO TRUST FRAMEWORK?

In Azure, the Zero Trust Framework is viewed as an all-encompassing solution to your security needs. In other words, a holistic approach is used so that your requirements can be met in the best way possible. To this extent, the Zero Trust Framework in Azure consists of the following components:

1) The Identities:

These are all of the entities that are trying to access the resources you have deployed in Azure. This not only includes the direct employees, but also the machines and other automated tools that also access them as well. This is what is called the "Zero Trust Plane" in Azure.

2) Devices:

This includes anything and everything that your employees use to access Azure. For example, this can be Internet of Things (IoT) devices, smartphones, notebooks, hard-wired desktop computer, tablets, and other forms of wireless devices.

3) Applications:

This not only includes the applications that you create in Azure, but also all of the Microsoft Office-based products that are available in M365. The goal here is to ensure the following:

- Shadow IT Management is reduced as much as possible. This is where your employees download software applications that have not been authorized by your IT Security team.

- Ensure that the appropriate controls have been assigned when it comes to accessing any type or kind of application.

- Keeping out to the maximum extent possible abnormal or other suspicious types of behavior.

- Make sure that all changes made to the configuration of any software application is properly documented and conforms to the baseline that has been previously established.

4) Data:

All kinds and types of datasets must be classified, labeled, and encrypted. This includes anything and everything from Data At Rest to Data In Motion to Data Processing, and even Latent Data and Personally Identifiable Information (PII) Datasets.

5) Infrastructure:

The Zero Trust Framework must be deployed to all Azure platforms which includes Infrastructure as a Service (IaaS), Platform as a Service (PaaS), and Software as a Service (SaaS). This even includes all of the applications you create, going as high as the level of Virtual Machine to the most granular level, up to the level of your source code.

6) Networks:

In Azure, the Network Infrastructure that you create is called the "VNet". The Zero Trust Framework in this regard should be able to do the following:

- Network Segmentation.

- Threat Protection.

- End-to-End Encryption.

The above is illustrated in the diagram below:

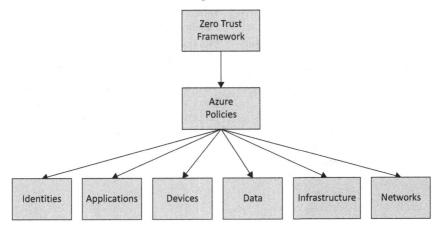

THE AZURE ZERO TRUST FRAMEWORK MATURITY MODEL

This methodology consists of the following components as depicted in the matrix below:

Component	Traditional	Advanced	Optimal
Identities	*On-premises identity provider is in use. *No Single Sign On (SSO) is present between cloud and on premises apps. *Visibility into identity risk is very limited.	*Cloud identity federation is present. *RBAC is enforced. *Use of analytics.	*No passwords are used. *User, device, location, and behavior are analyzed in real time.
Devices	*Devices are domain joined and managed with Azure Active Directory. *Devices are required to be on a segmented network to access data.	*Registration of all devices. *Least Privilege is enforced. *Strong security policy for Bring Your Own Device (BYOD).	*Endpoint detection is further used. *Access control used on BYOD devices.
Applications	*On-premises apps are accessed through Virtual Private Network (VPNs). *Mission critical resources only to those who have authorization to access them.	*Two Factor Authentication (2FA) or Multifactor Authentication (MFA) is enforced. *Mission critical applications are closely scrutinized.	*Least privilege is strongly enforced. *Dynamic control is also implemented.
Infrastructure	*Safe configuration of the Virtual Machines (VMS) and the workloads running on them. *Privileged Access Management (PAM) permissions are assigned with close scrutinization.	*Workloads are closely monitored for malicious behavior. *Every workload is properly identified. *Just In Time access is used.	*Unauthorized deployments are blocked. *Granular visibility and access control are available across all workloads *Access segmentation is enforced.

Component	Traditional	Advanced	Optimal
Network	*Minimal amount of network perimeters. *Static traffic filtering accomplished. *Encryption of network traffic in Azure.	*Micro segmentation is used. *Content filtering is used. *Internal traffic is encrypted.	*Ingress/egress monitoring is enforced. *AI and ML are used for threat detection and filtering. *All network traffic is encrypted.
Data	*Sensitivity labels are applied to all datasets	*All datasets are classified. *Encryption is also deployed.	*AI and ML are used to develop classification schemes. *Security policies dictate access control. *The above can be shared as long as Encryption is in place.

The Azure Zero Trust Framework Maturity Model is illustrated below:

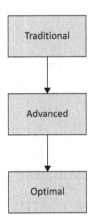

AN OVERVIEW OF THE TOOLS IN AZURE FOR ZERO TRUST DEPLOYMENT

In order for you, the Chief Information Security Officer (CISO) and your IT Security team to deploy the Zero Trust Framework into Azure, use of the following components is highly suggested. They are also available in Azure:

1) Ensure the strongest levels of authentication:

This is where the role of MFA must be used for authentication and threat detection.

2) Policy-Based Success:

Deploy the right kinds of engines that are available in Azure so that the correct kinds of security policies as they relate to authentication and access can be properly enforced.

3) Microsegmentation:

Make sure that all of the applications you create have their own segmented layer of security and MFA.

4) Automation:

Use the available ML and AI tools to help automate the routine and mundane processes in your Azure Cloud deployment.

5) Use AI:

Make use of this sophisticated tool to track abnormal behavior in real time so that you can respond quickly.

6) Data:

Discover, classify, protect, and monitor all of your datasets with AI and ML so that this will greatly mitigate the risks of data exfiltration, whether it is intentional or not.

THE IMPLEMENTATION OF UNITED STATES FEDERAL GOVERNMENT STANDARDS IN THE AZURE ZERO TRUST FRAMEWORK

To prove the validity of the Azure Zero Trust Framework Maturity Model, the following government standards have also been implemented:

1) The National Institute of Standards and Technology (NIST):

The NIST document that drives this is the NIST Special Publication 800-207. This document provides further guidance on how to craft a Zero Trust Framework in Azure, based upon your own security requirements.

2) Trusted Internet Connections:

This is a collaborative Zero Trust Framework document that is offered by the Office of Management and Budget (OMB), the Department of Homeland Security (DHS), Cybersecurity and Infrastructure Security Agency (CISA), and the General Services Administration (GSA).

3) Continuous Diagnostics and Mitigation:

This is created and implemented by CISA. It offers guidance on how to deploy the Zero Trust Framework for the following Azure components:

- Dashboarding.

- Asset Management.

- Identity and Access Management.

- Network Security Management.

- Data Protection Management.

UPDATES TO THE AZURE ZERO TRUST FRAMEWORK MATURITY MODEL

The following matrix depicts the latest updates:

Verify Identity	Verify Device	Verify Access	Verify Services
*Strong levels of identity confirmation are used. *Biometrics are strongly favored over passwords. *Least Privilege is now enforced to the highest standards possible.	*The health of all devices now is closely monitored and enforced. *Infrequently used devices have covert methods of being logged into. *Users do not have PAM level privileges.	*Safe Internet connections are now the default standard. *Subnetting is now based upon RBAC and functionalities.	*RBAC is now strictly enforced. *Only secure and safe connections are permitted into the Azure Portal.

THE OTHER ASPECT OF DEPLOYING THE ZERO TRUST FRAMEWORK IN AZURE

So far in this book, we have looked at all of the technical implications of deploying the Zero Trust Framework into Azure. Yet, there is still one other critical factor that needs to be taken into very serious consideration. This is the human, or social aspect of deploying it. As has been stated many times in this book, the basic crux of the Zero Trust Framework is to never trust anybody, even those who have been with you the longest.

In this regard, your employees may take serious offense at this (of not having any level of implicit trust). In fact, this can be a huge turn-off, and thus you may not get employee buy-in for the deployment of the Zero Trust Framework. As much as the technical side of it is important, so is this social aspect. After all, if your own employees are not supportive of it, then there will be of course a strong resistance to it, because the Zero Trust Framework is by all definitions an extreme way of authentication and authorization. So therefore as the CISO, as much as you need to gauge how you will deploy the Zero Trust Framework into Azure from the technical side, you also need to assess how your employees will react to it.

This can be done by using the concepts of the Technology Acceptance Model (TAM). It is reviewed in more detail in the following subsections.

THE TECHNOLOGY ACCEPTANCE MODEL—AN OVERVIEW

The most famous one has been the one that was created by Fred Davis, for his doctoral dissertation. This has become known as the Technology Acceptance Model (TAM). It simply states that the adoption of a particular IT system is dependent upon two key variables:

- The perceived Ease of Use of the System.

- The perceived Usefulness of the System.

It can be diagrammed as follows:

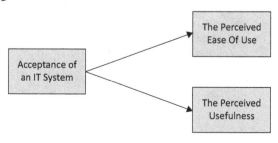

So, as one can see, a quick adoption of an IT system is dependent upon how the end user (in this case the Remote Worker) feels it is easy to use, and how much more productive it will make them in not only their current job, but also even in their daily lives.

It is important to note at this point that an IT system can be defined as any piece of hardware or software package that the end user either wishes or needs to adopt quickly, over a short period of time. But before we do a deep dive into Technology Acceptance, it is first important to define what adoption really is, and some of the other major theoretical frameworks that have led up to the creation of the TAM.

THE DEFINITION OF TECHNOLOGICAL ACCEPTANCE

Based on the literature, adoption can be technically defined as follows:

> Technology acceptance is about how people accept and adopt some technology for use. User acceptance of technology has further been explained as the demonstrable willingness within a user group to employ IT for the tasks it is designed to support (Dillon 2001). Therefore, acceptance can be viewed as a function of user involvement in technology use. Acceptance can be further described as the critical factor in determining the success or failure of any technology and acceptance has been conceptualized as an outcome variable in a psychological process that users go through in making decisions about technology (Dillon and Morris 1996). Technology is of little value, unless it is accepted and used.
>
> *(Source: G D M N Samaradiwakara, MLS, BSc, C G Gunawardena, PhD, MA, BA. "Comparison of Existing Technology Acceptance Theories and Models to Suggest a Well Improved Theory/Model". International Technical Sciences Journal (ITSJ) June 2014 edition Vol.1, No.1.)*

Breaking this definition down further, here are the key components of it that merit further attention:

1) There must be some sort of willingness by the end user (such as the Remote Worker) to fully adopt the IT system for use. It is important to note that this must be of free will, and it cannot be forced upon the end user. Also, the IT system must be adopted in its whole or entirety, it cannot be adopted in bits and pieces.

2) Acceptance can also be viewed as the final make or break for the IT system, after it has been developed, procured, and implemented. If it has not been adopted by free choice and in its entirety, then the entire IT system will go to waste.

3) The above point is further substantiated by the last point made in the definition. After all, the bottom line is why create something if it will not be accepted?

4) It has also been hypothesized that if an IT system is adopted in its entirety by the will of free choice, then more information and data will be demanded from it, thus pushing it to its maximum and optimal levels that are possible as set forth by the specs of the IT system.

THE THEORETICAL FORMULATIONS FOR THE TECHNOLOGY ACCEPTANCE MODEL

The TAM is deeply rooted in previous models and theoretical frameworks. Below are some of the major models that have led to the credence and establishment of the TAM:

1) The Cognitive Dissonance Theory (CDT):

The CDT is used to explain how discrepancies (dissonance) between one's mindful cognition and reality can change the person's subsequent cognition and/or behavior. It is important to note that the bulk of this theory comes from the end user's preset expectations of the IT system, assuming they know what a particular system is about, to varying degrees.

2) The Innovation Diffusion Theory (IDT):

The IDT is used to describe the innovation–decision process, which is largely fueled by the adoption of the IT system by the end user. The primary intention of this model is to provide an account of the manner in which any technological innovation moves from the stage of invention to its widespread deployment and use.

3) The Task Technology Fit (TTF) Model:

The TTF model holds that an IT system is more likely to have a positive impact on individual performance and can be used if the capabilities of IT match the tasks that the user must perform. In other words, if the end user (such as the Remote Employee) feels that the system is helping them to a great extent in achieving their daily objectives, then the IT system will be accepted almost immediately, with no hesitance involved. This model is composed of eight key variables:

- Quality.
- Locatability.
- Authorization.
- Compatibility.
- Ease of use/training.
- Production timeliness.
- Systems reliability.
- Relationship with the end users.

4) The Expectation–Disconfirmation Theory (EDT):

The EDT model focuses in particular on how and why user reactions change over time, when it comes to the final acceptance of an IT system. This particular model consists of four main constructs:

- Expectations.
- Performance.
- Disconfirmation.
- Satisfaction.

5) The Theory of Reasoned Action (TRA):

The TRA model has been deemed to be the first to gain widespread acceptance in technology acceptance research. It is a versatile behavioral theory and statistically models the attitude–behavior relationships. This theory maintains that individuals would use a particular IT system if they could see that there would be positive benefits (outcomes) associated by fully adopting and using them.

6) The Theory of Planned Behavior (TPB):

The TPB model is deemed to be a successor of the TRA model and it introduced a new variable known as Perceived Behavior Control (PBC). It is determined by the availability of skills, resources, and opportunities, as well as the perceived importance of those skills, resources, and opportunities to gain specific outcomes. In other words, the statistical probability that a person will intend to do a desired action can be increased by the quick adoption of a particular IT system.

7) The Social Cognitive Theory (SCT):

The SCT model is based on the notion that environmental influences such as social pressures or unique situational characteristics, cognitive, and other personal factors including personality as well as demographic characteristics key factors in the total adoption of an IT system. Additional variables have been included in this model, which include the following:

- Gender.

- Age.

- Experience.

8) The PC Utilization (MPCU) Model:

The underpinning paradigm in the MPCU model is the theory of human behavior. In other words, the model predicts the adoption and utilization of an IT system based upon end user utilization behavior. The primary function of this model makes it particularly suited to predict ultimate IT system acceptance and use across a wide range of IT systems.

9) The Motivational Model (MM):

The MM examines the key variable of Extrinsic Motivation and Intrinsic Motivation as it relates to the adoption of an IT system.

10) The Decomposed Theory of Planned Behavior (DTPB):

The DTPB models key variables of Attitude Belief, Subjective Norm (social influence), and PBC and decomposes them into specific belief dimensions of:

- Perceived Usefulness (PU).

- Perceived Ease of Use (PEOU).

- Compatibility.

The first two serve as the primary variables for the first version of the TAM, which is now discussed in the next section.

THE TECHNOLOGY ACCEPTANCE MODELS

As the title of this section implies, there actually have been three different versions of the Technology Acceptance Model. The first was created by Fred Davis.

1) The Technology Acceptance Model (TAM):

This was the first model to make full usage of pure psychological variables which affect technology acceptance and out of all of the models just reviewed in the last section, the TRA model that forms the backbone of the TAM model. This model states that the variables of PU and PEOU ultimately determine the adoption and usage of an IT system, with the Intention to Use (Attitude) serving as the Mediator Variable of actual system use. Further, PU is also seen as being directly impacted by the PEOU.

This is illustrated below:

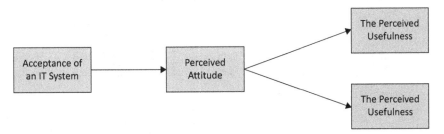

2) The Technology Acceptance Model (TAM2):

This second model of TAM is a theoretical extension of the original TAM model to address the following:

- The impacts of Social Influence and Cognitive Instrumental processes.

- How the effects of these determinants change with increasing user experience over time with the fully adopted IT system.

3) The Unified Theory of Acceptance and Use of Technology (UTAUT):

The UTAUT is deemed to be the third version of the original TAM model. This greatly enhanced model consists of eight new variables, which are as follows:

1) Performance Expectancy.

2) Effort Expectancy.

3) Social Influence.

4) Facilitating Conditions.

5) Gender.

6) Age.

7) Voluntariness.

8) Experience.

HOW TO ADAPT THE TECHNOLOGY ACCEPTANCE MODEL FOR THE ZERO TRUST FRAMEWORK IN AZURE

Now that we have provided a solid background to the TAM, we can now illustrate how it can be applied to the Zero Trust Framework in Azure, in terms of employee acceptance. It can be illustrated as follows:

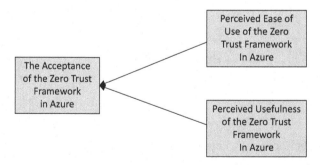

A TENTATIVE SURVEY

In this section, we propose the constructs for a potential survey in order to gauge just how the employees of your business view the ultimate deployment of the Zero Trust Framework in Azure. The components of the survey are as follows:

For the Perceived Ease of Use of the Zero Trust Framework

1) I often become confused with all of the Cyber authentication information and data I am receiving on a daily basis.

2) Because of the lack of clarity of the authentication information and data that I am receiving, I overlook the alerts and warnings I receive on a daily basis.

3) Trying to understand the Cyber authentication information and data that I am receiving is quite difficult.

4) I need to consult with others on my team to discern this Cyber authentication information and data.

5) It takes a lot of mental effort to break down the Cyber authentication alerts and warnings that I am receiving.

6) It is easy to recover from any mistakes that I make from the Cyber authentication information and data that I am receiving.

7) The Cyber authentication information and data that I am receiving is hard to apply to the Cyber Threat Landscape.

8) The Cyber authentication information and data that I receive produces results that I am not expecting.

9) I find it very tiresome and cumbersome to try to triage the Cyber authentication information and data that I am receiving.

10) My daily interaction with the Cyber authentication information and data that I am receiving is easy to deal with.

11) The Cyber authentication information and data that I am receiving produces a more secure environment for my employer.

12) The Cyber authentication information and data that I am receiving guides me in helping to predict the future Cyber Threat Landscape.

13) Overall, I find that the Zero Trust Framework is easy to use.

For the Perceived Usefulness of the Zero Trust Framework

1) It would be difficult to perform my everyday job tasks without the Cyber authentication information and data that I am receiving.

2) Having access to Cyber authentication information and data gives me a greater control in helping to secure my environment.

3) Using effective Cyber authentication information and data helps me to improve the overall Cyber hygiene when I conduct my daily job tasks for my company.

4) The Cyber authentication information and data I am receiving address the needs for the job that I am doing.

5) Having Cyber authentication information and data allows me to accomplish my work-related tasks, which is protecting my company from any Cyber threats.

6) Having Cyber authentication information and data supports the mission critical aspects of my daily job functions.

7) Having Cyber authentication information and data makes me spend less time on other activities which may require higher levels of security.

8) Having Cyber authentication information and data improves the overall level of effectiveness that I doss on my job.

9) Having Cyber authentication information and data improves the quality of the work that I do on my job.

10) Having Cyber authentication information and data increases the productivity levels of my job.

11) Having Cyber authentication information and data makes it easier for me to do my job.

12) Overall, I find that having the Zero Trust Framework is useful for my job.

The above survey will use a ranking scale of 1–5, where the value of "1" indicates "Highly Agree" and a value of "5" indicates "Highly Disagree". This is illustrated below:

1 = Highly Agree	2 = Moderately Agree	3 = Neutral	4 = Moderately Disagree	5 = Highly Disagree

A MULTIPLE REGRESSION MODEL OF THE ZERO TRUST FRAMEWORK IN AZURE

This is represented as follows:

$$AZTF = \beta PEOUZTF + \beta PUZTF$$

Where:

AZTF: Acceptance of The Zero Trust Framework

$\beta PEOUZTF$: Perceived Ease of Use of the Zero Trust Framework

$\beta PUZTF$: Perceived Usefulness of the Zero Trust Framework

CHAPTER 4

Conclusions

In summary, this book has examined the following:

CHAPTER 1

* * The Cyber Risks of BYOD.

* * The Mobile Device Management Plan.

* * The Benefits of a Mobile Device Management Plan.

* * The Components of a Good Mobile Device Management Plan.

* * The Evolution of Cloud Based Deployments.

* * The Disadvantages of On-Premises Infrastructure.

* * A Review of the Cloud.

* * The Three Cloud Platforms.

* * The Major Cloud Deployment Models.

* * The Benefits of the Cloud.

CHAPTER 2

* * The Cybersecurity Models.

* * The Lockheed Martin Cyber Kill Chain.

* * The Diagram of the Lockheed Martin Kill Chain Model.

 DOI: 10.1201/9781003442578-4

* The Diamond Model of Intrusion Analysis.

* The Diagram of Diamond Model of Intrusion Analysis.

* The Attack Graphs.

* The Diagram of the Attack Graphs Model.

* The MITRE ATT&CK Model.

* The Perimeter Defense Model.

* Unimodal Authentication.

* Two Factor Authentication.

* Multifactor Authentication.

* Using Biometrics in Multifactor Authentication.

* The Zero Trust Framework.

* The Advantages of the Zero Trust Framework.

* How to Deploy the Zero Trust Framework.

CHAPTER 3

* How the Zero Trust Framework Is Embraced by Microsoft Azure.

* The Use of Policies.

* What Is Included in the Azure Zero Trust Framework.

* The Azure Zero Trust Framework Maturity Model.

* An Overview of the Tools in Azure for Zero Trust Deployment.

* The Implementation of United States Federal Government Standards in the Azure Zero Trust Framework.

* Updates to the Azure Zero Trust Framework Maturity Model.

* The Other Aspect of Deploying the Zero Trust Framework in Azure.

* The Technology Acceptance Model—An Overview.

* The Definition of Technological Acceptance.

* The Theoretical Formulations for the Technology Acceptance Model.

* The Technology Acceptance Models.

* How to Adapt the Technology Acceptance Model for the Zero Trust Framework in Azure

* A Tentative Survey.

* A Multiple Regression Model of the Zero Trust Framework in Azure

Finally, the Cloud is the way to go, whether it is provided by Amazon Web Services (AWS) or Microsoft Azure. It offers so many more benefits and advantages versus On-Premises Infrastructure, as was reviewed in this book. Also, the way of the traditional security models (as also reviewed in this book) will be far too outdated over time to have any meaningful purpose to businesses in Corporate America. This especially holds true for the Perimeter Defense Model.

This has its inherent set of weaknesses, such as once the cyberattacker breaks through this only line of defense, they will have access to everything. All kinds and types of cyberattacks can happen here, ranging from Ransomware to Identity Theft to the worst yet, Data Exfiltration. It is important to keep in mind in this aspect that the cyberattacker of today has become extremely covert, stealthy, and ultra sophisticated. As was examined in this book, gone are the days of the "Smash and Grab" campaigns. The cyberattacker of today is now taking their time to study their unsuspecting victims, even using openly available tools such as Open Source Intelligence (OSINT) and Social Media sites, as well as other types and kinds of resources that are also freely available on the Internet.

In order to combat all of this and keep the cyberattacker at bay, a new kind of Cybersecurity Model has to be created and deployed, which is the Zero Trust Framework. Although there is really nothing new about its concepts, its deployment has been just recent. This is an extreme kind of model, in that nobody can be trusted, each and every entity must be constantly verified, whether it is a human being or even a machine, such as a Chatbot.

As businesses move more into the Cloud, deploying the Zero Trust Framework will become of even more paramount importance. While the other Cloud Providers have provided some means of deploying this kind of framework, it is Microsoft Azure that has surely come to the forefront in this regard. There has been constant research and development done in this area, and as a result, the tenants that make use of Microsoft Azure will have the latest tools at their disposal for deploying the Zero Trust Framework, not in just a quick and efficient manner, but also in one that will provide the maximum levels of security to the newly found Cloud-based Infrastructure.

But also keep in mind that as much as deploying the Zero Trust Framework is a technical feat, so are the psychological aspects of it. For this reason, it is very important for you, the Chief Information Security Officer (CISO), to gauge just how willing your employees will be in using the Zero Trust Framework. True, you could just mandate its use, but that will not serve any purpose. You want your employees or end users to feel comfortable and at ease when using it, and they should not by any means feel forced to use it. This only lessens its ultimate acceptance.

Finally, keep in mind that the Zero Trust Framework is not a "one size fits all" kind of model. It has to be configured to your exact security requirements. Not only do you not need to create the plan for it, but it should also be tested at each and every step of the way. It should not be deployed all at once, but rather it should be deployed in distinct phases so you will be assured that all of the components are all working seamlessly together.

In the end, you should also use Multifactor Authentication for your newly deployed Zero Trust Framework. You should always try to steer away from using Two Factor Authentication. If possible, Biometric Technology should be the primary authentication mechanisms that are used in this regard, as they will provide the highest levels of authentication and authorization than any another mechanism (such as usernames/passwords, challenge/response questions, RSA Tokens, or even One-Time Passwords).

Index

Printed in the United States
by Baker & Taylor Publisher Services